THE ULTIMATE
BUCKET LIST

THE ULTIMATE
BUCKET LIST

50 BUCKETS YOU MUST SEE BEFORE YOU DIE

DIXE WILLS

ICON

Published in the UK in 2020
by Icon Books Ltd, Omnibus Business Centre,
39–41 North Road, London N7 9DP
email: info@iconbooks.com
www.iconbooks.com

Sold in the UK, Europe and Asia
by Faber & Faber Ltd, Bloomsbury House,
74–77 Great Russell Street,
London WC1B 3DA or their agents

Distributed in the UK, Europe and Asia
by Grantham Book Services, Trent Road, Grantham NG31 7XQ

Distributed in Australia and New Zealand
by Allen & Unwin Pty Ltd, PO Box 8500,
83 Alexander Street, Crows Nest, NSW 2065

Distributed in South Africa by
Jonathan Ball, Office B4, The District,
41 Sir Lowry Road, Woodstock 7925

Distributed in India by Penguin Books India,
7th Floor, Infinity Tower – C, DLF Cyber City,
Gurgaon 122002, Haryana

Distributed in the USA
by Publishers Group West,
1700 Fourth Street, Berkeley, CA 94710

Distributed in Canada
by Publishers Group Canada, 76 Stafford Street, Unit 300
Toronto, Ontario M6J 2S1

ISBN: 978-178578-680-8

Typeset by Marie Doherty

Printed and bound in Great Britain by Clays Ltd, Elcograf S.p.A

To the Mayflower crew, without whom this book
would probably still have been written.

Introduction

Unassuming, perennially overlooked and yet nigh
on universal, the bucket is the ultimate unobtrusive
onlooker, the fly on the wall sat in quiet contemplation
at all the great turning points in world history. Blessed
with a design of such simplicity and brilliance that it
has remained unchanged over the millennia, the humble
bucket possesses a versatility unmatched in the history of
human invention. Fill it with sand and you've got a fire
extinguisher – perfect for putting out fires of any size up
to and including small candles. Fill it with ice and you've
got a charity challenge spread by social media. Fill it with
water and you've got yourself a bucket of water.

Not to be confused with its exotic coal-portering
cousin the scuttle, the bucket is happy in all its known
states: empty, not quite empty, encrusted with a lining of
concrete, upside down, 'partially filled with radiation from
one of daddy's experiments which is why, children, you
must never touch the cat again' and verminous. And hey,
unlike a sandwich, you can fill a bucket with an infinite
amount of anti-matter and you've got the makings of
your very own portable black hole, complete with its own
event horizon, Schwarzschild Radius and handle.

It's now widely accepted that in the Middle Ages as
much as 90% of all matter not classified as 'general filth
and disease' was rags. What's less well known is that the

other 10% was bucket. Though it's obviously upsetting that the canny little vessel now plays a less prominent rôle in daily life, popular culture still teems with references to buckets and pails. Jack and Jill (p29) famously made an incident-packed assault on a hill to fetch one; while the difficulties attendant in using straw to mend a hole in a bucket are discussed at some length by a punishingly dreary couple named Liza and Henry.

Popular bucket-centred phrases include President Truman's famous dictum 'the bucket stops here'; the ubiquitous business cliché 'there's no 'I' in bucket'; and the meteorologist's favourite 'it's bucketing down', an expression that saw its genesis after the Great Bucket Storm of 1731 in which Hemel Hempstead was almost entirely destroyed by a freak storm of buckets. Visit the town today and you'll see why God chose to smite it.

But perhaps the best-known idiom of all is 'to kick the bucket', a somewhat louche summation of the snuffing out of a fellow human being's life. It's commonly believed that its origins stem from hangings in which the unfortunate subject falls from or is pushed off a bucket. However, this is all tosh and should be expunged from your mind, leaving room for other things like the details of the collapse of the Ottoman–Turk Empire.

The most likely explanation is that the saying derives not from the modern bucket as we know it but from the days when the term was used to define a yoke or beam (as is still the case in Norfolk, the land that time forgot). In the process of being slaughtered, pigs were customarily suspended on such yokes and, in their last desperate struggle for the life cruelly being taken from them by a so-called higher species, were apt to 'kick the bucket'.

Out of this phrase crawled 'the bucket list', an inventory of activities curated by folk who fear that there will come a day when they cease to exist. Death is, as we know, nothing more than fake news put about by the lame-stream media as part of an eco-fascist scam run by George Soros from a secret lair deep inside the Hoover Dam. However, for those who let themselves be taken in by the lie, the prospect of not being around any more provokes a perfectly natural urge to bungee-jump off the roof of the Sistine Chapel and dash headlong into the Caspian Sea to go swimming with artichokes. It's the ultimate in FOMO.

This is all well and good but, as we all know, when it comes to the ultimate in fulfilling life experiences, you really can't beat a good viewing of a bucket. In this assertion I am backed by philosopher, polymath and scourge of the milquetoast Thomas Hobbes who sunnily observed that life is 'solitary, poor, nasty, brutish, and short, so you may as well pack in as many buckets as you can before it's over'.

To that end, for the first time since the Ancient Babylonian scroll of *Interesting Pails That May Not Be Available In The Afterlife*, this book corrals details of the planet's 50 best buckets to view, see and otherwise run an appreciative eye over. From the Aboriginal and Torres Strait Islander People Kelp Water-Carrying Bucket to Hedy Lamarr's Bucket of Spread Spectrum Frequency Hopping Bits (and Bobs), all history's top buckets are here, along with a selection of surprisingly compelling contemporary buckets specially chosen for the connoisseur who prides themself on keeping abreast of the hot new models in the never-less-than-exhilarating world of buckets.

Each entry comes with useful information on where to go to see the bucket in question. And last but not least (in fact, at the front), there's a handy list of the 50 buckets to tick off until you've got the set and can die as peaceably as nature allows.

Happy Bucketing, one and all!

And don't forget – if you die before seeing all 50 you've totally failed at life.

* * *

For those readers who find the concept of kicking the bucket too distasteful, there's my companion volume *Shuffling Off – 50 Mortal Coils You Must See Before You Conk Out.*

The Ultimate Tickable Bucket List

Tick each bucket off by popping a tick in each bucket. The countdown to the end of life has seldom been more fun.

1 Cleopatra's Bucket

2 Moon-Landing Rock Sample Bucket

3 Marie Antoinette's Milking Pail

4 The Original KFC Bucket

5 The Bromeswell Bucket

6 The Bucket Wheel

7 The Bucket of Blood

8 The Basilewsky Situla

9 Mi'kmaq Birchbark Maple Syrup Bucket

10 Jack and Jill's Pail

11 Ashurnasirpal's Protective Spirit Bucket

12 Van Gogh's Bucket

13 Agatha Christie's Apple-Bobbing Bucket

Consolatory bonus box 🪣 – tick this if you die before you see all 50 buckets.

THE ULTIMATE
BUCKET LIST

Cleopatra's Bucket

Much tosh has been written about the meeting of Cleopatra and Mark Antony in Tarsus in 41 BC. However, insiders know that once they'd had a chat about the spelling of Antony's name and what had happened to the h and all that (he didn't know – it had always 'just not been there'), they found they didn't have much to say. Also, Latin was an Indo-European tongue while Egyptian was Afro-Asiatic and there was not a lot of common ground, to be honest.

Inevitably, the conversation turned to buckets.

'Nice bucket you've got there,' Antony ventured. This date hadn't gone as he'd hoped. Bucket-chat was very much Plan C territory. To aid comprehension, he pointed at the bucket and smiled.

'Thank you,' Cleopatra replied. 'It's for transporting the asses' milk to my bath from … well, from that container over there.'

She mimed a servant dipping the bucket into that container over there and transporting the milk to her bath. She cringed. Why were they even in her bathroom? She couldn't for the life of her work out how that had happened and she began to wonder if there hadn't been a misunderstanding. Well he needn't think he was going to go in here. Roman general or no, he could use the communal palace toilets like everyone else.

'Fascinating,' said Mark Antony, unfascinated. This was all going terribly. Here he was, a third of the triumvirate. What did that make him? A triumvirile? A triumph? A trumpet? Anyway, pretty much the most powerful man in the Roman Empire meeting the woman who could fund a whole military expedition if he fancied having a crack at the Parthian Empire, *which he very much did, yes please thankyouyesindeedyesyes*. And yet they were pointing at a bucket – *o me miserum*.

'What?' asked Cleopatra. But she was already thinking longingly of an asp.

■ **SEE IT:** *Great Mimes Through Time*, Tarsus Museum, Turkey.

Moon-Landing Rock Sample Bucket

Everyone knows Neil Armstrong's famous first line on taking his one small step for him upon the surface of the Moon. (Why such a small step, Neil? You weigh almost nothing suddenly – have a good old stride.) The second line, uttered by Buzz Aldrin, was less memorable but all the more gladdening for being unscripted.

'Have you got the rock sample bucket, Neil?' he buzzed, for they were on first-name terms.

'Bother!' quoth Neil, somewhat more vexed than his exclamation might imply but aware that his words were still being broadcast to untold millions below. 'Could you get it from the space cupboard, Buzz?'

There was no such thing as a space cupboard on Apollo XI – it was just an ordinary cupboard – but after his gaffe, Neil was keen to regain the admiration of the untold millions below. Buzz clambered back in the spacecraft – his unmic-ed expletives lost to posterity – and fetched the bucket.

Unlike the cupboard, the bucket was no run-of-the-mill object. It had had to be devised specially in a NASA workshop by a whole team of experts – far more indeed than would normally design a bucket. The vessel had to be tailored to the lunar atmosphere and so its bottom and sides had been freighted with space lead, which was just ordinary lead but with a cool name and which cost over a thousand times as much because otherwise Team Bucket knew they wouldn't be taken seriously. They spent three years devising a handle that wouldn't let the bucket sort of drift about when it was carried and thus look silly when the untold millions below saw it on their small televisions.

It was only after lift-off that one of the team realised they should probably have added a lid.

■ **SEE IT:** Kennedy Space Center, Florida, USA (do ask to see the recreation of the Team Bucket expenses spreadsheet).

Marie Antoinette's
Milking Pail

We've all been there. Whether it's while reversing a tractor near the edge of a cliff-top or bringing Flight BL472 in to land from our seat in the control tower, we've all let our minds drift off into a dream world where we can at last fulfil the one true desire of our heart: to play at being a dairy maid.

It's a reverie one is susceptible to even if one is queen of France (which so few of us are nowadays). Of course, if you are queen of France (don't get your hopes up – see previous parenthesis for details) and also possess a fantastically cavalier attitude to the nation's coffers, you can make that dream a reality. If you're Marie Antoinette (see above), you needn't confine yourself to one dairy but can splash out on a pair (one in which the cheese, butter and cream are made, and a second in which to wolf down same – nom nom) and construct a whole hamlet around them.

Naturally, with all the poor around her happily munching away on cake, she wasn't going to stint on the assorted accoutrements needed for playing dairy maid. The ruby-encrusted milking stool has been lost to posterity, along with the solid gold butter churn paddle. Thankfully, the royal milking pail is still with us. The persistent rumour that it was fabricated from human skin donated by obsequious courtiers, though compelling in its imagery, is likely to be untrue. Philosopher-comedian Jean-Jacques Rousseau reported, possibly in jest, that the pail looked 'a bit human-y'. However, in all probability, like most royal milking pails of the time, it was simply made of peasant.

■ **SEE IT:** Palace of Versailles, Versailles, la belle France. At the ticket office, repeat the following phrases: '*Où sont la crème, le beurre et le fromage? Ils sont dans la bouche de la reine. Reine gloutonne!*'

The Original KFC Bucket

'Our fragments of fried chicken shrapnel are still too appetising.'

It was a balmy summer's day in 1957 when Leon Weston 'Pete' Harman sat on his back lawn pondering how to save the American people from themselves by weaning them off the food-like product careening out of his restaurant. His was the first-ever franchised Kentucky Fried Chicken outlet and, if Leon Weston 'Pete' Harman had his way, it would be the last.

Over the picket fence, his neighbour carelessly watered a pair of oversize concrete mushrooms. Leon Weston 'Pete' Harman forced his head down into his hands and let flow a stream of hot and bitter tears. It simply seemed beyond all hope and expectation to make the shards of fried chicken projectile any less appealing.

Even he did not know the terrible secret of Colonel Sanders' '11 herbs and spices' recipe but he assumed that at least four of the ingredients were proven emetics if taken in large enough doses.

'Pull yourself together, Leon Weston "Pete" Harman,' he told himself angrily. 'Is this the same man who launched The Do Drop Inn?' And he *was* the same man who launched The Do Drop Inn. Or at least co-launched it with his wife Arline.

He looked around for inspiration. His neighbour was still watering the mushrooms. That's it! He'd serve the stuff up in a watering can!

No. Too classy. What's not at all classy?

'A bucket! A bucket!' He would have his servers sloosh the splinters of fried chicken grenade into a bucket. Nobody who wasn't utterly depraved ate from a bucket. 'And I'll make the bucket out of grass. No, stamps! No! …'

'Cardboard,' he breathed at last. 'Loathsome loathsome cardboard.'

Relaxing back into the lawn, a smile crept across his chiselled face. 'KFC,' he murmured to a passing raccoon, 'KFC would be dead by Christmas.'

■ **SEE IT:** Harland Sanders Café and Museum, Corbin, Kentucky, USA.

The Bromeswell Bucket

I t's a truth universally acknowledged that, given enough time and rainwater, crops and animals will both pretty much grow unassisted. As a result, and despite what they might tell you, farmers have very little to occupy their time once they've finished listening to *The Archers*. Bored beyond all human telling, they often resort to poking about in the mud and slurry of their farms. It's no surprise, therefore, that some of Britain's most beloved ancient treasures – the Gemmed Horns of Bazminster, the Kelmswick Silver Muesli, the Hatchworthy Spasms – have all been discovered by our agricultural friends.

One such yeoman, stabbing the earth one day in 1986 in a state of ineffable ennui, came across the Bromeswell Bucket. To a great extent he was cheating, since he was at Sutton Hoo, site of an almighty Anglo-Saxon ship burial and 'folk cemetery' (i.e. where folk were buried). The 6th-century bronze vessel was manufactured in Turkey and features naked Nubian swains toughing it out with lions beneath a Greek inscription that reads, 'Use this in good health, master count, for many happy years.' As you might expect, it had once been a gift from a Roman army bigwig to a Barbarian king, and was full of the ashes of a deceased Anglo-Saxon (presumably added at a later date).

It's a damning indictment of modern Western society that the tradition of bucket-giving has almost completely died out. This Christmas, why not revive some of that good old Roman army munificence by giving your nearest and dearest a bucket? Imagine little Tommy/Judy's eyes brimming with tears of exultation as they rip open the wrapping paper to reveal a bucket inscribed with some pithy Greek epithet.

'Thank you, mummy! Thank you, daddy!' the little cherub will cry, 'I can't wait to use it. Can we cremate you now?'

■ **SEE IT:** National Trust Visitor Centre, Sutton Hoo, Woodbridge, Suffolk.

The Bucket Wheel

All the world's best innovations have been accidental. The bicycle, the electric tin opener, blood – they all came into being because of a mishap, fluke or unlikely twist of fate. But the greatest invention of all occurred because of an incident involving the humble bucket.

Our tale concerns two Mesopotamian neighbours. Their names are lost to us so for ease of narration we'll call them Biff and Biff. Biff was a fastidious man. He cleaned his cave at the coming of each gibbous moon and always gave his stick a wipe before lancing his boils. However, his neighbour Biff liked to play practical jokes.

'I don't do them for their own sake,' he explained to Biff, 'but to illustrate the absurdity of life.'

So came the day that Biff, feeling the need to remind his well-ordered neighbour of the folly of existence,

placed a bucket of unknown origin outside Biff's door. Early the next morning, as Biff emerged from his cave, he stumbled on the bucket which, falling over, proceeded to roll across the alluvial plain towards the Euphrates (or the Tigris – it's not known which). Biff watched transfixed. Nothing before had ever rolled in quite the way this bucket rolled.

'Thank you, Biff!' he called to his neighbour, who was lurking behind the tusk pile, shoulders quaking with mirth.

And straightways Biff set to work. He invented the axle, then another one, affixed four sideways buckets and named them 'wheels' because nothing else had that name yet. He invited the still chuckling Biff to sit on the trolley's freshly-crafted platform and, without further ado, rolled him into the Tigris (or the Euphrates – it's not known which) where he promptly drowned.

Biff returned to his cave. All of a sudden, life didn't seem absurd at all.

■ **SEE IT:** El Museo de Cosas Redondas (Museum of Round Things), La Ronda, Spain.

The Bucket of Blood

'What you got there then, landlord?'

The proprietor of the only pub in the Cornish village of Phillack was drawing water from his well. Startled, he turned round sharply.

'Said what you got there, landlord?'

It was the captain of the local revenue men. Drat the fellow. The landlord smiled with apparent unconcern.

'Cat got your tongue?' asked the captain with an undertone of menace.

'No, no, Captain Rakes – you … you surprised me, is all,' stuttered the landlord. 'Lovely day, is it not? You still out looking for poor young Jack what was kidnapped and foully mutilated by they terrible smugglers?'

The captain ignored the question. 'Something amiss with your well, landlord? Water seems awful dark to me.'

The landlord let slip the handle, the bucket dropped and the two men heard a curious *thump* – as when bucket meets mutilated body.

'Butterfingers!' exclaimed the landlord. 'Anyway, mustn't keep you from your work.'

'Haul it up, landlord,' said Captain Rakes, his hand caressing the handle of his holstered pistol. And up rose the bucket again, full of blood.

'Care to explain?'

'Bah! That darn bush, scusing my language!' cried the landlord. 'It does grow down there so prodigious strong as would pull the eyes out of a ferret. It's no business turning my well water thick and red with its cranberry fruit. Mind you, I'll say this, it's very good for the cystitis – cleared mine right up.'

'Well, as you were then, landlord,' said the captain cheerily. 'I'd give that bucket a good wash, mind. Some folks be allergic to cranberry.'

And so it came to pass that, sometime later, the name of the pub was changed to The Bucket of Blood. Because it *was* blood, you know. Mutilated bodies don't bleed cranberry juice. Not even in Cornwall.

■ **SEE IT:** Bucket of Blood, Phillack, Cornwall (do tell the staff about any food allergies before ordering).

The Basilewsky Situla

Everyday folk have *buckets*; the gentry have *pails*; archaeologists and high church folk have *situlas* (while people with a smattering of Latin and a penchant for pedantry have *situlae*). And that's just the English speakers. Let's not even mention Hungarian which has 23 words for *bucket*, the choice of which depends on the contents of the bucket, the status of the user in relation to the bucket, and whether the bucket is suspected of being self-aware. Such buckapartheid™ is one of the key reasons the human race is doomed as a species.

As Nature abhors a vacuum, so the Priesthood abhors a bucket. 'If one must put holy water in a container (and one really must or it will evaporate, putting it at risk of being breathed in by a passing heathen),' the Priesthood laments en masse, 'then at the very least make that

container a situla. Oh, and make it pretty so it doesn't resemble a b*ck*t. Amen.'

The Basilewsky Situla was made of ivory (tsk tsk) around 980 in honour of the German Holy Roman Emperor's trip to Milan. It's fair to conclude from this that, if you've visited Milan and no one has thought to create a situla to commemorate the event, you're doing life wrong. Ditto if your chosen career path fails to ensure your job title will someday include the word emperor.

This particular situla is adorned with a dozen scenes from the passion and resurrection of Christ, a smidge of 5th-century hexameter and two human heads. These last have had holes bored right through them to hold the handle. Dr Freud, come on down.

■ **SEE IT:** Victoria and Albert Museum (Medieval & Renaissance, Room 8, The William and Eileen Ruddock Gallery, case 15), London. The museum apologises for not being able to give more precise directions.

Mi'kmaq Birchbark Maple Syrup Bucket

If there's anything the Mi'kmaq people enjoy, when sitting around the Maritime Provinces of Canada, it's a good word game.

'Stoke up the fire,' one Mi'kmaq person might say to another, 'and let's devise a new lexicon based on the different sounds one might make on eating a lemon.'

The fire duly stoked, ball-points poised and ready between fingers almost too febrile with excitement to compose with the legibility the game demanded, the fun would begin.

One night, during a particularly vicious ice storm in Clam Bay, Nova Scotia, two Mi'kmaq folk hit upon a word game that would steer the often capricious course of Bucket History in new directions.

'I'm calling this one Say Any Three Nouns at Random and Then Make That Thing,' one said.

In other countries, this might lead to truly absurdist creations, such as a coypu biscuit telescope. In Canada, however, there are only nine things: maple syrup, ice storms, trees, buckets, birchbark, poutine, Mounties, moose and void (lemons, though known about in Canada, are widely believed to be mythical). Thus, when the two Mi'kmaq friends had completed their game, which went:

'Birchbark! Your turn.'
'Maple syrup! Your turn.'
'Bucket!'
(In chorus) 'Top game!'

it was an outcome that was not wholly unpredictable. What is perhaps more surprising is that the bucket in question turned out rather well and that birchbark proved to be a first-rate medium in which to carry maple syrup. Up until that time (3 March 1990), the tree-tapped sap had had to be carried in the hands, which is why Canadians were known as a sticky-pawed folk whose handshakes were to be treated warily and whose hugs were to be avoided at all costs. Indeed, it is thanks solely to the birchbark maple syrup bucket that Canadians are now on the verge of acceptance into wider society.

■ **SEE IT:** Moose Poutine Void, Dartmouth, Nova Scotia.

Jack and Jill's Pail

For centuries, buckets were the preserve of the common people. Posh folk could never be seen carrying something so vulgar as a bucket and consequently, whenever they had need of one, were compelled to call upon an apothecary/chamberlain/cordwainer/scullion/scrofula-infested monger of some sort to wield the container on their behalf. Seeing a gap in the market, seasoned bucket manufacturer Jeremiah Groat rebranded his top-of-the-range model a 'pail', a corruption of the word 'palaeontology'. In a flash, so-called 'pail parties' became fashionable among the social elite. These would involve a variety of pail-based games, the most popular being a mixed-sex race to the summit of a specially created knoll.

The craze was captured in a popular contemporary nursery rhyme:

> Jack and Jill
> Went up the hill
> To fetch a pail of water
> Jack fell down
> And broke his crown,
> And Jill came tumbling after.

Crowns, which were worn continually by the monarchs of the time, were notoriously fragile and would often snap on contact with a knoll or even a hummock. Such breakages were taken as a sign of divine displeasure by the common folk who would instantly parade the maladroit sovereign upside down through their scrofula-infested streets. The regal head was then plastered with vinegar and brown paper and struck from the body with a halberd or, if there was no halberd to hand, a guisarme.

No fewer than fourteen European heads of state were overthrown after games of 'Jack and Jill' in the 16th century alone. This rose to a peak of three a month in 1664, after which the sport was banned in favour of a new game called Bubonic Plague (see 'Ring a Ring o' Roses').

■ **SEE IT:** Jeremiah Groat Museum of Buckets, Pails and Cholera, Bamako, Mali.

Ashurnasirpal's
Protective Spirit Bucket

As anyone who was there at the time will tell you, the forces of chaos were a right hassle in 9th-century BC Assyria. Any Assyrian king worth his salt was understandably keen to defend himself from said agencies, while one of them, Ashurnasirpal II, grew particularly averse to disorder of any kind. His collection of sun-dried bricks was arranged in alphabetical order, and he made everyone at his main palace in Nimrud wear a lanyard featuring a depiction of their face, carved by a top local artist, and a barcode, just in case there happened to be a breakthrough in scanner technology during his lifetime.

Being a belt-and-braces kind of despot, he took pains to build chaos-protection into the very walls of his palace. The gypsum panels in his throne room were thus adorned with bird-headed spirits holding a bucket and cone. The spirit would dip the latter into the former (or at least would have done so had the engraving come to life for some reason) and splash a sort of magical purifying liquid about the room, setting up a force-field the shadowy instruments of bedlam could not penetrate. And it worked too – Ashurnasirpal II reigned for 24 years, allowing him to visit chaos on myriad others, enslaving and genociding all over the place.

Thankfully, bird-headed spirit protection isn't just for 9th-century BC Assyrian kings. To ward off the forces of chaos today, simply purchase a bucket, cone and magical purifying liquid from your usual supplier and employ a bird-headed spirit to get splashing (most now accept contactless payment). Unless you like a bit of chaos, of course, in which case move to Leicester.

■ **SEE IT:** Ashmolean Museum, Oxford. (Hurry because the museum is super keen to return the bucket-based panel to chaos-free Iraq. Probably.)

Van Gogh's Bucket

'Urgh!'

Doutzen awoke in her trundle bed and contemplated the day ahead without enthusiasm. This would be her … she counted on her abnormally short fingers … *ninth* consecutive day modelling for Vincent. What had started as 'oh just give me a couple of hours for a quick sketch, Doutzie' had turned into a marathon of half-finished scribbles.

First she had had to sit in a chair. Then she had to stand behind the chair. Then the chair 'just wasn't working'. The chair was ditched for a sunflower, then several sunflowers, then, for reasons he never went into, a room of people eating potatoes.

'What is tiredness?' he had goaded her, 'when I am going to make the name of Doutzen van Niemand immortal.'

He had made her sit in a café, then outside on a starry night ('not enough stars' he'd sighed), then again on a starry starry night ('too many stars').

'Fame, Doutzie! Stardom everlasting!' he had called out as he compelled her to dig in a snow-covered field. (She had had to supply the snow herself. And the field.)

She had posed beside Dr Rey; behind Dr Rey ('sorry, couldn't see you – I've only painted Dr Rey'); up a cypress; with a bandage over her ear; and in Arles ('Arles? Vincent, Arles is 200 miles away.' 'Immortality, Doutzie, immortality!').

At length, on the ninth day, Doutzen fell to her knees. Exhausted beyond all human telling, she grabbed a bucket in which to be sick.

'Hold it!'

And at last Vincent was satisfied. His pencil sped deftly across the paper.

'What are you going to call it, Vincent?'

'Oh, I don't know – "Girl kneeling in front of a bucket" probably.'

■ **SEE IT:** As illustrated opposite. If anything, this one's an improvement on Van Gogh's 'Girl kneeling in front of a bucket' which, to be honest, would be better without the sick.

Agatha Christie's
Apple-Bobbing Bucket

It's no secret that the biggest-selling author of all time was obsessed by buckets. However, she also rigidly adhered to Chekhov's dramatic principle: 'If you say in the first chapter that there is a rifle hanging on the wall, in the second or third chapter it absolutely must go off.'

It was for this reason that, for many years, the Queen of Mystery heroically kept buckets from appearing in her work, knowing only too well that, if they did, every single murder thenceforth would involve a bucket, or multiple instances of bucket. In 1969, she finally cracked. Later claiming to have been distracted by a blackbird, or multiple instances of blackbird, she absentmindedly inserted an apple-bobbing bucket into the first chapter of the Hercule Poirot mystery *Hallowe'en Party*. Eight pages later she'd drowned an entire child in it. The floodgates were open.

Halfway through her next novel, an experimental Miss Marple/sci-fi mash-up to which she'd given the working title *Ten Thousand Buckets of Death*, her publisher intervened. As a result, the stirring tale in which the canny spinster's village of St Mary Mead is over-run by a legion of robot buckets controlled by an evil alien genius named Percule Hoirot was forever denied an airing. The uncompleted manuscript was burnt in a fireplace along with a beeswax candle and a Sumatran blowpipe, although these were later discovered to be red herrings.

Since Christie's death in 1976, there have been over a thousand fan fiction versions of *Hallowe'en Party*. Only one of them, penned by a teenage Irvine Welsh, is worthy of attention. The apple-bobbing bucket becomes '… the biggest bucket of skag in the history of buckets. And skag.' The entire population of Edinburgh drowns in it, possibly in a dream sequence.

■ **SEE IT:** The best apple-bobbing bucket action takes place in the early chapters. It's downhill after that.

Harold II's Bucket Helmet

I f only Harold Godwinson had read Sun Tzu's *The Art of War.*

'Only a fool rushes headlong into battle,' China's greatest military strategist begins, 'wearing a helmet he has made from an upturned bucket. The blacksmith may be a surly fellow and his prices verging on the criminal but he does know how to make a helmet. Sadly, you do not (unless you are also a blacksmith).'

On 14 October 1066, Harold II of England faced a canny foe: the Normans. Not since the days when the Goths, Visigoths and Quentins scared the *lorem ipsum* out of the Ancient Romans by posing more of an attacking threat than their name suggested has a people group used its unassuming moniker to such advantage. Also, they had perfected the art of making arrows that were not only easy on the eye but literally eye-catching.

But all that would have counted for nought had it not been for Harold's decision to eschew the standard issue Anglo-Saxon helmet in favour of an upturned bucket of his own design. As is clearly shown on the Bayeux Tapestry, when Harold is forced to release the bucket in order to attend to the arrow in his eye, the handle just sort of flops over his nose in a highly unmilitary fashion.

Harold's death sealed his army's doom at Hastings, a battle habitually viewed by the English as a rare defeat followed by an unbroken string of storming victories from Bannockburn to Dunkirk. However, there was a considerable upside: the manner of Harold's death gave birth to a French phrase used to convey heartfelt thanks: '*Merci buckets.*' The expression remains, to this day, the only two words of French ever learnt by the English.

■ **SEE IT:** Battle Abbey's *Buckets At War* exhibition (open alternate Tuesdays, concessions half price, take your shoes off at the side entrance).

Paul Revere's Bucket of False Teeth

Ask any American who Paul Revere was and you'll
get the same answer over and over again: 'He's
America's greatest living dentist.'

But who was Revere? And how? Happily, the second
question is easy to answer. Like so many of America's
heroes, he was the son of a Frenchman. A silver shop
proprietor, he came so close to bankruptcy in 1765 that
he was forced to become a dentist.

Instantly rich (his wealth was so admired by his
countryfolk that the verb 'revere' passed into the English
language), he joined the fight against the British, a nation
whose teeth have seldom been on good terms with a
dentist. To reach his patients, Revere was known to ride

great distances on his horse Penobscot, often at night – still the gods' favourite time for visiting dental pain on mortals. His tooth-whitening procedures were so effective that they're credited with winning the Battle of Concord where rebel colonists famously overcame yellow-fanged British troops by smiling at them repeatedly until they were blinded.

But Paul Revere (a man whose campaign for enhanced oral hygiene so horrified the British that the verb 'appal' passed into the English language) will always be best known as a hero of socialised medicine. He roamed the land with his famous bucket of false teeth fashioned from bits of discarded walrus (the teeth, not the bucket, which was probably made from tea solidified by Boston harbour sea salt) and for absolutely no charge fitted his fellow separatists with imitation gnashers. He thus created the original fake smiles behind which Americans would go on to conquer the whole world parts of Samoa.

■ **SEE IT:** Dr. Samuel D. Harris National Museum of Dentistry, Baltimore, Maryland. Understandably, the Bucket of False Teeth is kept under the tightest of security. When museum officials pretend that they've never heard of it, use the password 'Paul Revere was a Communist traitor' and you'll definitely get some action.

The Pythagorean Bucket

It's a commonly held misapprehension that all buckets are, give or take a stylistic tweak or two, roughly cylindrical. However, you need only go back 2,500 years to discover that the prevailing bucket shape of the day was in fact a parallelogram. This had been developed by Ancient Greek prop forward Anaximander, who loved parallelograms and made all manner of household utensils in that shape, including mops, bladder skewers and slaves.

Since Greece was the super-power of the day, the parallelogram swiftly became the standard form of bucket throughout the known world, despite obvious issues vis-à-vis stability and, as Execrable of Thebes was to lament in his work *On the Properties of Shapes and Liquids*,

'… matter just sort of slopping out of it, like a drunk Minoan.'

Into this listing atmosphere strode Pythagoras, destroyer of hegemonies, donner of sheets. Still buzzing from his discovery regarding the sum of the squares on the two shorter sides etc. etc., Pythagoras was, as contemporaries later described him, 'triangle happy'. He invented triangular bricks, triangular wine and even isoscelean forms of abstract nouns, which caused quite a rumpus among devotees of Euclid, as can be imagined. But the apotheosis of his golden age was without doubt the Pythagorean bucket. He teamed up its revolutionary 'no handle' design with a triangular base and three triangular sides that met at a point at the top. Critics from the area bordering Judea and Egypt who observed that this was just a pyramid and that there was 'no opening to put anything in' were summarily hurled from the peak of Mount Athos. Philistines.

■ **SEE IT:** According to legend, the original Pythagorean bucket was lobbed into the volcano of Santorini in order to appease Hermes, the Greek god of missing packages. However, plenty of the so-called 'School of Athens' Pythagorean buckets, some of exceptional quality, can be viewed at the Pythagoras Mechanical Workshop Museum, Norrtälje, Sweden.

The Great Fire of
London Bucket

As any English person will tell you, the Great Fire
of London of 1666 was the only fire in history
whose details are worth committing to memory. Having
the good sense to occur in a '66 year, the conflagration
joined the only other two dates taught in English schools:
1066, when the English lost the Battle of Hastings (find
out why on p41) and 1966, when Camberwick Green
became the first BBC television programme filmed in
colour.

The Great Fire also had the wit to start and end in
memorable places – the blaze famously broke out at a
bakery on Mind Yer Backs Street and ended in Fizzle
Alley. What is less often recalled is why the fire was not

extinguished at the bakery in the first place. Thankfully, an early black box recorder (a grey parrot, who happily survived the inferno) captured the scene and was able to reproduce it verbatim at the ensuing inquiry.

'Eberneezah!'

'What now?'

'Them scones is looking unco burnt and, well, fiery.'

'They's not burnt, Methoos'lah, they's just black. Customers likes 'em with a bit of black on – masks the flavour o' the jam.'

'Yes, why *does* plague jam taste so strong o' rat?'

'Enough o' your fernickiting – go fill that bucket from the river and douse them scones.'

[Sounds of grumbling. A five-minute pause. The noise of timbers crackling.] (The parrot was a famously skilled operator and went on to do a ton of radio work.)

'Right here you go …'

[Sounds of a bucket being swung.]

'That put 'em out, Meth?'

'Not so's you'd say, Eb. Bucket was empty – got a ruddy 'ole innit.'

'You wash your mouth out, my girl.'

'I would if I could get some water to do so. Oh and by the way, mind that—'

[Assorted screams, a crash.]

—fireball.'

Transcription ends. The parrot is thanked for her help.

■ **SEE IT:** The Monument, Conflagration Street, London.

Hedy Lamarr's Bucket of Spread Spectrum Frequency Hopping Bits (and Bobs)

Paul Winchell, the ventriloquist who provided the voice for Tigger in Disney's *Winnie-the-Pooh*, is also the inventor of an artificial heart. Canadian singer Neil Young has sold tens of millions of albums and rhymed 'black' with 'that', but also holds seven patents relating to model trains. (So your excuse for not finding a cure for cancer because 'you've been quite busy at work lately' simply doesn't hold water. Pull your finger out, slacker.)

But the queen of all the world's brilliant-at-this-but-also-a genius-at-that folk is Hedy Lamarr.

After fleeing Austria, Lamarr met MGM-head Louis B. Mayer, became 'the world's most beautiful woman' and was soon a huge Hollywood star. Being a self-taught scientist, she also redesigned billionaire aviator Howard Hughes' planes to make them go faster, and in 1942 developed a frequency hopping spread spectrum system to prevent the Axis powers jamming the radio waves that guided Allied torpedoes. Since she was a civilian, the US Navy refused to adopt it, which was why the war went on for so long. Also, they queried her use of a bucket to keep all her spread spectrum frequency hopping bits and bobs in. She's on record as having 'winked and, seconds later, exploded' – apparently in a successful bid to divert her questioners' attention.

Lamarr's techniques went on to be used in early forms of Wi-Fi and remain a vital element of Bluetooth technology. More importantly, her legacy also lives on in the form of her son, the singer Limahl, and his son, the singer Lemar.

■ **SEE IT:** The National Women's History Museum and the National Inventors Hall of Fame (both Alexandria, Virginia, US) take turns in displaying the bucket, which is ceremoniously carried through the streets from one to the other every Monday at 1pm, accompanied by duetting bagpipers.

Henry I's Bucket
of Lampreys

'Fetch me yon bucket!' Henry's squealy (but because monarchical still a bit fear-making) voice rang out over the forest of Lyon in sunny Normandy.

Every duke, earl and courtier knew to which bucket the king referred and gave a collective sigh.

'And stop that confounded sighing, you caddis-gartered snivelfest.'

This really impressed them because 'caddis-garter' was not to become a term of abuse for another 500 years and even then exclusively as a noun. A hush fell upon the assembly.

'Well come on!'

The lamprey boy, wiping a cold sweat away with his darndel, rushed sovereignwards with a freshly-filled bucket of the eel-like parasitic fish. It was the king's third bucketful and it was still officially breakfast.

A physick, braver than even the knights of the company, leapt at once from his seat. 'Your majesty! I fear thou art in mortal danger. Dost thou not know that a man may expire from a surfeit of lampreys?'

'A what of lampreys?'

'A *surfeit*, sirrah.'

'And what's that when it's at home?'

'It's, err, *too many*, your highness.'

'So put that whole sentence together for me again?'

'A surf—'

'Without using *serfit*, dolt-pedal.' A titter went around the tables – the king had said 'pedal', which sounded potentially rude.

'A too many of lampreys, sirrah.'

'*A too many of lampreys*,' Henry mocked. 'Never heard so much rot in all me life – and I'm 67, or possibly 68, no one seems to know.'

And before the next lamprey had wriggled down his throat (he liked them *very* fresh) he was dead. Because he'd had enough of experts.

■ **SEE IT:** Following Henry's death, Normandy became awash with counterfeit 'royal lamprey buckets' that changed hands for anything up to two cows. Thus if you travel to the region today, you'll find almost every householder owns one and will swear that theirs is the genuine article. Agree swiftly and leave before it gets ugly.

Big Bank Hank's
Bucket Hat

O ur stay on this chunk of rock hurtling through
space is scarily brief, which is presumably why we
choose to spend so much of it staring at screens in a
bid to anaesthetise ourselves to the hassle of existence.
However, some folk find themselves distracted for
long enough to contemplate what it might be like not
to be here anymore. This can spark a desire to achieve
immortality through the creation of a Great Work.

Some draw buckets next to girls (see p35); some
distribute free teeth (p45); while the most intelligent
seek deathless fame by writing books to be read on the
loo. In Big Bank Hank's case, he achieved immortality on
three fronts. Unable to turn his degree in oceanography

into a relevant job, he instead rapped Grandmaster Caz'
memorable lyrics (there was quite a lot of hippieing
to the hop and boogieing to the bang involved) on
'Rapper's Delight' by the Sugar Hill Gang. In so doing,
he performed on the world's first hip-hop hit *and* starred
in the world's first hip-hop music video. If this were
not enough, he was single-handedly responsible for the
resurrection of the bucket hat, as seen atop his head in
said video.

Created in the early 1900s to keep the rain off Irish
farmers and fishermen, and later adapted for sporting by
US troops in Vietnam and mods in Brighton, the bucket
hat had left the building until Hank came along. The rest,
as they say, is history. Pretty much everyone on the planet
now wears bucket hats, from Rihanna to fans of defunct
Beatles tribute act Oasis. Indeed, anyone not wearing a
bucket hat is now viewed as deeply suspect and is liable to
be denied their daily food ration.

■ **SEE IT:** Big Bank Hank sadly left us in 2014. Keep his
star alive by watching the video for 'Rapper's Delight' on
repeat night and day. *Do not get distracted.*

Baseball's Imaginary Bucket

Tell any American that some cricket matches last five days only to end in a draw and they'll look at you with complete incomprehension. Many will become aggressive and may attempt to strike you on your nose and hair. This is because things that take too long or which are not certain to end with a victor and a vanquished are deemed un-American and contrary to all Americans' God-given right to be bankrupted by an uninsurable pre-existing illness.

Take baseball, for instance. Like all sports popular in the US, baseball is mostly adverts. These are occasionally interrupted by outbreaks of throwing, stick-swinging and running about. Since Americans are church-going folk, an organ plays at all times to remind both fans and players that soon it will be Sunday. However, unlike a church service, a game of baseball will not last for five days and there will be a result. This is mainly due to the rôle played by imaginary buckets.

Not stepping into a bucket is sage advice in any situation, but in baseball even more so. When learning to bat, children (known in America as 'kids' or 'grist') often fear getting hit by the ball, flung at them by the jug (or 'pitcher') and so step backwards to avoid any damage to their brain likely to cause a pre-existing illness. They are thus taught by their coach to imagine that a bucket has been placed behind them by person or persons unknown. Should they 'step into the bucket', this person or persons unknown will kill them and eat them. No one wants to be killed and eaten, so the child opts instead for the pre-existing illness. Uncle Sam rejoices. The American Dream lives on.

■ **SEE IT:** Baseball is played on a continuous loop everywhere in America at all times. This is why it rankles that they always get beaten by Cuba. Squint while staring at the batwielder and the imaginary bucket will materialise behind them.

The Bobrinski Bucket

These days, increasing numbers of people are ringing me up at my unlicensed surgery and saying, 'Why on Earth can we no longer buy buckets that have Hollywood-style credits on, like what you used to in them old days? The old days were better. Among other things, we had Spangles. And also, a future.'

They speak the truth, these increasing numbers of people: the old days *were* better. And what better illustration of it do we have than the Bobrinski Bucket? Created in 1163 for a merchant who lived in Herat (now part of Afghanistan), the bronze vessel provides the canvas, if you will, for one of the earliest surviving instances of Persian anthropomorphic calligraphy. The credits read:

Orderer
'Abd al-Rahman ibn 'Abdallah al-Rashidi

Inlayer
Muhammad ibn 'Abd al-Washid

Artist
Mas'ud ibn Ahmad, the decorator of Herat

For its owner the brilliant Rukn al-Din, pride of the merchants, the most trustworthy of the faithful, grace of the pilgrimage and the two shrines, Rashid al-Din 'Azizi ibn Abu al-Husain al-Zanjani, may his glory last.

Nowadays, if you got one of your people (you have people, right?) to order a bucket for you and, when it arrived, it was engraved with credits along those lines, you'd probably feel pretty jazzy about yourself. But it was in fact the artist who was the real winner here, because Mas'ud ibn Ahmad was asserting his intellectual property rights over the design.

'So why,' my callers go on to cry, 'is it called the Bobrinski Bucket and not the Mas'ud ibn Ahmad Bucket?'

'Because,' I tell them, 'Count Alexey Alexeyevich Bobrinski, a descendant of Catherine the Great, just happened to acquire it.'

And that, my friends, is why the artist will always be the first to starve.

■ **SEE IT:** The State Hermitage Museum, St Petersburg, Russia.

Jan and Dean's
Bucket Seats

Did the 1960s produce two greater life forms than Jan Berry and Dean Torrence?

As with any question of that nature, the answer is no. Obviously. For Jan and Dean not only sang songs about surfing and songs about souped-up cars, but also songs like 'Surfin' Hearse' that were about surfing *and* souped-up cars (and unwitting nocturnal visits to cemeteries). Their 'Schlock Rod (Part 1)' and 'Schlock Rod (Part 2)' have been verified by scientists as the two finest pieces of music ever created by humankind. As a result, the One World Government (those conspiracy theorists were right all along, which is why they're being targeted with chemtrails to shut them up) has the two songs on constant standby to be played as a sign of peace to any extra-terrestrial forces that threaten to invade the planet.

But Jan and Dean will always be best known for their love of bucket seats. In their 1964 waxing 'The Anaheim, Azusa and Cucamonga Sewing Circle, Book Review and Timing Association' the bucket-shaped car-fitting is lauded as a prime locale for 'shooting the breeze'. However, it's the song 'Bucket "T"', their paean to a hot-rodded version of the Ford Model T, that sees their obsession with the bucket seat given full rein. Released as a B-side to 'Batman!', the track remains one of the few flip-sides to reach the giddy heights of number 66 in the US Billboard while featuring the word 'bucket' sung over 150 times. Just weeks later, Jan Berry suffered a near-fatal car crash near Dead Man's Curve in Beverley Hills. Coincidence? Or the work of shapeshifting alien reptoids? You decide.

■ **SEE IT:** The Museum of Jan and Dean has three branches – in Anaheim, Azusa and Cucamonga – but the One World Government has made their precise locations known only to the Illuminati.

Emily Brontë's
Wuthering Bucket

'Out on the wily windy moors, we'd roll and fall in green.'

These, of course, are the memorable opening words of *Wuthering Heights*, Emily Brontë's semi-gothic novel of love, jealousy, gender inequality and wind. One of six ill-fated siblings, Emily and sisters Charlotte and Anne amused themselves by writing stories and staying alive. But with her sheltered upbringing in isolated Haworth, where the only man she knew was her brother Branwell, Emily was never exposed to normal boys' names.

To get around this, whenever she needed to name a male character in a novel, Emily wrote random words on a sheet of paper, taking inspiration from her surroundings

– the heath, say, or a hare she had seen while out fetching oats and laudanum for Branwell, or some lint. She then tore said parchment into strips and threw them into what she jokingly referred to in her journal as her 'wuthering bucket':

'*Wuthering* because when I take it outside to fetch oats and laudanum for Branwell the wind curls itself up inside it making such a roaring sound as would like to terrify me if I were the terrifying sort. *Bucket* because it is a bucket.' Two strips drawn out of the bucket at random furnished her with a name.

Hence *Wuthering Heights* is populated by men with the Christian names Hind-ley, Hare-ton, Lint-on and, famously, Heath-cliff. After the author's death, her publisher attempted to mask the oddity of the names by removing the hyphens.

In Emily's honour, the word *wuthering* was retired from the English language, and has never been used since.

■ **SEE IT:** Brontë Parsonage Museum, Haworth, Yorkshire. The Brontë's former home has an enviable collection of buckets belonging to all three literary sisters. On payment of a nominal extra fee, visitors can write their own random words and throw them in the bucket. These are then distributed among local schoolchildren as a treat at Michaelmas.

Mr Creosote's Bucket

Of all the films produced by Monty Python's Flying Circus, their 1983 offering, *The Meaning of Life*, is arguably the most unhinged. And of the random selection of sketches somewhat tentatively held together by the gossamer thread of the film's theme, the most memorable features the truculent and sensationally obese Mr Creosote.

The late Terry Jones, who wrote the sketch and played the eponymous anti-hero, knew that the quickest way to an audience's funny bone was via a bucket. Thus, as soon as he is seated at his table in the restaurant, he declaims, 'Better get a bucket, I'm going to throw up.' And from there on in, it is the bucket rather than Creosote that takes centre stage, which accounts for the sketch's enduring appeal. The vessel produced for Creosote's prodigious emesis is a fine one – a classic galvanised zinc model (see p119). Soon, this is so full that another bucket is produced. This follows a well-known comedy rule: 'One bucket elicits laughter, but two are flipping hilarious.'

But the bucket as comedy fail-safe really comes into its own after [*SPOILER ALERT*] Mr Creosote's explosion, when a racist cleaning lady fills it with vomitus while reciting a poem about not having learnt anything about the meaning of life from cleaning some of the great academic institutions.

Terry Jones' bold and pioneering allegory has had quite the legacy. Bucket sales instantly went through the roof – 1983 is still viewed as an *annus mirabilis* among manufacturers and retailers. Some countries have even introduced so-called 'double bucket' laws requiring citizens (and even tourists) to keep at least two buckets close to hand in case of emergency. Furthermore, creosote is now almost universally banned. Because it explodes.

■ **SEE IT:** After filming, all the props from *The Meaning of Life* were thrown into the Gorge of Eternal Peril, a location for which it is almost impossible to get travel insurance.

Isaac Newton's Bucket Argument

Calculating the global number of arguments centred around buckets over the millennia has never been an easy task. Some historians have suggested it could be between 2 and 3 million; more conservative observers have put it below 500; while many refuse to put a figure on it at all, which is both wise and cowardly at the same time. Uber-French philosopher Jean-Paul Sartre famously posited that there was 'no such thing as a bucket', thus creating the paradox of an argument about buckets in a universe devoid of the very subject of the argument. Pull the Gauloise out of that one.

However, perhaps the most famous bucket-related contretemps occurred when Sir Isaac Newton argued

about a bucket amongst himself. In his so-called Bucket Argument, he takes a bucket filled with water, hangs it up by a cord, twists the cord a good deal, lets it go, then watches the bucket whizz around. Although the water revolves at the same speed and in the same direction as the bucket, its surface gradually becomes depressed, as if struggling through a long and dark winter, and forms a perfect concave shape.

Now, while you or I might just have enjoyed looking at the pleasing form the water had taken before going inside for our tea, this wasn't enough for the apple-battered Newton who deduced all kinds of stuff from it. Most notably, he reasoned that the water was moving relative to absolute space. This is useful because back in the latter half of the 17th century, folk didn't think much about absolute space, preferring instead to indulge their mania for coffee houses and plague. Nowadays, of course, physicists say that the concept of absolute space is unnecessary because reasons. Still, it's nice to know it's out there.

■ **SEE IT:** Get a water-filled bucket. Whizz the bucket around on its own vertical axis. Witness physics. Go inside for your tea.

Larry Wright's Bucket Drums

I t's fair to say that the early years of Larry Wright's life were not easy ones. Born into poverty in the Bronx in the mid-70s, he was burnt out of his family's apartment at the age of five, began busking with a metal barrel to earn a crust a year later, spent his childhood drifting about in a nomadic semi-homeless existence, lost his mother in a drugs-related shooting and, perhaps most harrowingly of all, was then forced to carry, virtually single-handed, the first 85 seconds of *Green Card*, the Hollywood film that brought the world the on-screen pairing of Gérard Depardieu and Andie MacDowell, an experiment so bold and innovative that it was never tried again.

Widely cited as the originator of modern bucket drumming, when young Larry took to the streets with a five-gallon plastic bucket he'd liberated from a construction site near Times Square he was continuing a fine American tradition. During the Civil War, drummer boys as young as thirteen are reported to have 'played their dinner buckets like percussive instruments' as they bravely marched to their certain deaths. It's a detail that reveals perhaps the greatest depravity of that conflict: the use of buckets as dinner plates.

While still a teenager, Wright appeared in videos by Maria Carey and Fine Young Cannibals and a Spike Lee-directed advert for Levis. Had his life continued on this Hollywoodian rags-to-riches trajectory, he would by now have married Beyoncé at least once and be spending his weekends driving Bentleys into swimming pools and/or fermenting his own quinoa and flogging it as a meal-replacing superfood called *The Wright Stuff*. Instead, he busks, because that's what he likes to do. It's hardly the spirit, is it?

■ **SEE THEM:** Larry and his wife Sonia drum together at New York's Union Square, Penn Station, Port Authority, and 59th and Lexington subway stations.

Balti

'That bucket looks good enough to eat.'

We've all thought it at some point and, indeed, have probably all said it – though when you've said it you've always had that little laugh in your voice that betrays your true thoughts on the matter. Thank goodness there are some people in the world – we're looking at you, northern Pakistan – who are not so feckless. So enamoured are they with the gastronomic possibilities of the bucket that their favourite dish is just that: bucket (or, as they have it in Hindustani, Bengali or Odia: *balti*). Indeed, such is their devotion to the bucket that they have named their Chinese-border region *Baltistan* in honour of the plucky cylindrical portage vessel.

At some point in the 1970s, balti arrived in Birmingham, a place mainly famous for putting the 'blight' into Blighty. In those days, the people of Birmingham liked to eat straight from the bin, so this bucket-based cuisine, cooked in a wok-like cast-iron pan, was initially viewed as '*rairly* posh nosh'. As such, it was only eaten on the feast day of Dysfunctia, the patron saint of sludge, who was popular in a city whose inhabitants lived mostly in canals and for whom silt was considered a vegetable.

It was not long, however, before the doughty Brummies had been won over by the expatriate dish, eating it three or more times a day. The exclamation 'Balti gosht!' soon entered the vernacular along with the already firmly established, 'Rogan josh!' and, 'Shish kebab!' Myriad balti restaurants opened on Ladypool Road, Stoney Lane and Stratford Road. The area is known today as the Balti Triangle after the musical instrument traditionally played at each meal-time throughout the city to ward off hope.

■ **SEE IT:** Available in Pakistan's Baltistan region and the Balti Triangle, Birmingham. Despite the obvious marketing possibilities, the dish is not yet available in the Baltic.

Nicobar Islands Toiletries/Cosmetics Equipment Bucket

Almost nothing is made of spathe today. I'm sure I'm not alone in thinking that that's not only a waste but also a tragedy. For instance, you can trawl the cosmetics and toiletries departments of a thousand European stores and alight upon not a single spathe-made bucket designed for their safe conveyance. Even synthetic spathe receptacles have to be ordered from specialist dealers and paid for in krugerrands.

And yet the health benefits are potentially enormous. For decades, scientists have been telling us that daily interaction with the large sheathing bract that surrounds the flower cluster of certain plants (especially the spadix of palms and arums, of course) is vital for the correct functioning of our organs and feet. Indeed, ask almost any health-related question and if 'spathe' is not the answer, you're asking the wrong question.

Thank goodness then that the skills of spathecraft are being kept alive by the Nicobar Islanders. Not for them the collapsed spleen, the rotten lung or the hurty foot. When they luxuriate in their baths on their Indian Ocean archipelago, their toiletries/cosmetics equipment bucket – made entirely and exclusively of spathe – is on hand to suffuse their personhood with goodness and well-being (and to hold their toiletries/cosmetics, some of which may also be made of spathe).

Nowadays the Nicobar Islands are billed as a veritable paradise but life for the Nicobarese has not always been a spathe-made bowl of cherries. They have suffered earthquake, tsunami, rising sea-levels and, perhaps most distressing of all, colonisation by Austrians. Thankfully, the inhabitants have always had their spathe toiletries/cosmetic equipment buckets close by – an ever-consoling presence in times of trouble. We could all do with some of that.

■ **SEE IT:** Nicobar Islands, Indian Ocean (turn south on reaching the Andaman Islands).

Charlie Bucket

The eponymous hero of Roald Dahl's *Charlie and the Chocolate Factory* is a character widely revered (see p45) as the least obnoxious of the five children to tour Willy Wonka's chocolate factory, a trait that secured his inheritance of same.

What's lost on most readers is that Charlie Bucket's victory is the worst possible outcome imaginable. For Dahl's apparently breezy little morality tale is in fact his shot at doing *Animal Farm*. In common with Orwell's excoriating *roman à clef*, *C&CF* is a thinly veiled piece of agitprop railing against the movers and shakers behind the creation of the Soviet Union.

Wonka, needless to say, is Tsar Nicholas II, desperate to keep the hereditary principle in place. Augustus Gloop, the glutton sucked into a chocolate river, is clearly Lenin.

Trotsky is Veruca Salt, hurled into a garbage chute while being attacked by squirrels (this was Dahl's little joke – in Norwegian, the words for *squirrel* and *ice pick* are the same). Chewing gum addict Violet Beauregarde is Karl Marx, who is known to have become a huge inflated blueberry just days before his death. By turning Molotov into Mike Teavee, Dahl is practically screaming at his readership, 'Look! Could I make it more obvious? They've got virtually the same name!'

Chocolate itself is the opiate of the people; the golden tickets are something or other; and the Oompa-Loompas – who do all the actual work yet have no control over the means of production – are the umpen-lumpen proletariat.

Bucket's name is, of course, a none too subtle reference to the Yalta Conference Bucket (p147) and identifies him as Joseph Stalin, an opportunist who artfully manœuvres himself into position, takes everything over, and then runs it as his own personal fiefdom. We cannot say we were not warned.

■ **SEE IT:** Anywhere but Amazon, who ceased stocking the title after Jeff Bezos discovered that he himself was the garbage chute.

The Laminated Bucket of Fabius Amandus

Who'd be Fabius Amandus, eh? There he was, sitting in the atrium of his house in Pompeii in AD 79, looking at his table and his bucket and thinking how nice it was to be living in Pompeii in AD 79, what with all the modern conveniences like underfloor heating and a man on call night and day in case you had a headache and needed someone to drill a hole in your skull to let out the pain or the evil spirits or what-have-you. And now that he had his own table he could think about things to put on it, like stones or pebbles, or perhaps some nice rocks. Or maybe some dead things. There were always dead things lying about and perhaps some of them would look nice on a table. But, best of all, he had his bucket.

Not any ordinary bucket, either. No siree. For his bucket was laminated (Laminated! What would his father have said to that? Such times) and cylindrical and made of lead and decorated with signs of the zodiac, not that he believed in any of that, what with him being a Taurus.

And then he heard a man's voice calling outside in the street, 'Fabius Amandus!'

He ducked down – he had heard that chuggers were in town, raising money for diseased leopards. It was a good cause but he'd been feeling the pinch himself lately. That table didn't buy itself after all.

The man persisted. 'You know that massive great volcano we built our town next to?'

He thought he recognised the voice – it was the fellow who hired out kelp. He offered up a cautious, 'Yes …'

A pause. Just enough time, he thought, for the man to beat a silent drum roll in the air.

'Sjust gone off.'

■ **SEE IT:** House of Fabius Amandus, Pompeii. Turn left at the screaming family. Can't miss it.

Lord Buckethead

Lord Buckethead is not a real lord and his head is not made of bucket, both of which facts render it all the more extraordinary that he has become such a potent force on today's political hellscape.

Representing the *Gremloids* – his party name taken from the title of the Todd Durham film in which he came to prominence – Buckethead burst into the hearts and minds of the British voting public in the 1987 election. Never one to shirk a challenge, the probably fictional character only ever stands against sitting Conservative prime ministers. Thus he found himself facing off against Margaret Thatcher – the epitome of the evil nemesis – and came within just 21,472 votes of unseating her on the back of a popular pledge to demolish Birmingham (cleverly outflanked by Thatcher's pledge to destroy the

entire nation). So began a meteoric rise. In '92 he fell just 66.1% behind former person John Major.

But it was when constitutional changes directed that the UK hold a general election every six minutes that Lord Buckethead (not really a lord, not really bucketheaded) came into his own. In 2017 he amassed 249 votes, beating six parties and coming within an ace of overhauling Theresa May, albeit aided by major malfunctions in the latter's software.

At this point, everything went gremloid. Todd Durham contacted then Buckethead alter ego Jonathan Harvey and asserted his rights to the character, a move that would prove calamitous in all sorts of ways. In 2019, at the Uxbridge and South Ruislip constituency, Durham oversaw the candidacy of Lord Buckethead, while Harvey stood as Count Binface. With Buckethead, Binface and Alexander Boris de Pfeffel Johnson all contesting the seat, the silly vote was split three ways. Britain has never recovered since.

■ **SEE IT:** *Gremloids* is probably not showing at a cinema near you, so you'd be best advised to find the cinema furthest away from you and catch it there.

The Lady with the Bucket

'Flo, could you do a day shift tomorrow?'

'Sorry, sister?'

'Could you do a day shift tomorrow?'

'Well of course I can't.'

'Why ever not?'

'Because I'm *The Lady with the Lamp*! All the newspapers back in England say so.'

'Not that ag –'

'"– *Lamp in hand, she has become a ligth in the dakrest hour of our brave lads in far Grimea.*" That was the *Manchester Guardian*.'

'Well can't you carry your lamp around in the daytime?'

'Oh, I'll look a proper Charlie then, won't I, sister? I can just hear the patients now: "Why are you carrying a

99

lamp in daylight, Miss Nightingale?" "I never knew that lamp was surgically attached to your hand, nurse. Gurgle, gurgle, death rattle, death rattle." Can't you make Agnes do it? Her gimmick's a bucket.'

'Yes, that's not really working for her, is it?'

'Ha! I know. I went through all the papers last Sunday – not a word about *The Lady with the Bucket*. She's gutted.'

'Poor thing. What does she even have in it?'

'Blood, mostly, sister. Sometimes sinew. Thinks it makes her seem more down to earth – "woman of the people", that sort of thing – if she's carrying around a bit of blood and sinew.'

'Well, maybe I will put her down for the day shift then. No sleepless soldier's going to be cheered up by a bit of sinew.'

'Yes!'

Florence smiles and casually tosses some newspaper cuttings into the fire.

■ **SEE IT:** Imperial War Museum North, Manchester. Ask for 'that there bucket what that lady had in t' war. You know, that *long ago* war – not one of the famous ones, one o' them other ones that they fought anyway just because. You see you never know if your particular war's going to be a famous one or not and this one weren't. The lady with t' bucket in that one.'

The Bucket Toilet

Very much an item of technology that falls into the 'it's better than nothing' category – much like Windows 95, say, or the bagpipes – the bucket toilet can be seen anywhere around the world where public sanitation has yet to become a thing.

One of its great benefits, of course, is that it does away with fiddly stuff like plumbing (who's got time for that? it's hard to imagine even plumbers like plumbing) and sewage systems (ditto, but more so). For these reasons, the compact human waste receptacle is, in the vernacular of our times, massively hearted by 'preppers' – those folk with fully-stocked subterranean bunkers who will be laughing at us all when the Apocalypse does inevitably strike (at least they'll be chuckling up until the moment they realise that they're stuck with themselves

for the rest of their artificially extended lives and they've forgotten to dig a hole in which to empty their bucket toilet and they can't go above ground because the emergency radio station has told them the alien lizard army is still mopping up the last survivors of the carpet laser bombing from the space ships).

■ **SEE IT:** Better still, make your own and thus prepare yourself for the invasion of the alien lizard army (though strictly they're not lizards at all – that's just how life has evolved on planet X-50035199 and, had you been able to look closely before the lasers started up, you'd have seen they more closely resemble our friend the pangolin). You'll need a) a bucket b) a toilet seat c) someone who knows what they're doing who can stick them together properly so you don't, erm, have an accident (try asking Suzy – she used to date that bloke who turned his shed into a fortified command post).

Taylor Swift's *Bucket*

Taylor Swift (2006), *Fearless* (2008), *Speak Now* (2010), *Red* (2012), *1989* (2014), *Reputation* (2017), *Lover* (2019). Taylor Swift has banged out a new album consistently every two years since her eponymous debut. Except once – note that suspicious-looking *three-year* lacuna between *1989* and *Reputation*.

Although it's always been taken for granted that the extended gap was caused by Kanye West constantly interrupting TayTay's recording sessions by ringing her up with questions about Swedes ('What do they rhyme with?' 'Do they make good pets?' 'How many to a box?'), the real reason is even darker. It turns out that *Reputation* had to be hastily thrown together after Swift's decision to can her scheduled 2016 offering, the concept album she'd dreamed of recording ever since she was a child: *Bucket*.

The waxing was based on *The Bucket*, a much-loved short story by Gogol in which a lower-middle-class school inspector from Novobsk awakes one morning to find that someone has entered his chicken coop in the night and moved his bucket slightly to the left. As one might expect from the daughter of Irish satirist Jonathan Swift, the material Taylor wrote for the album took Gogol's classic pastiche of tzarist hegemony and ran with it, mercilessly sending up the madness and foibles of modern-day America. Songs written for the album included 'Reality TV Stzar', 'You're Such A Nazissist' and 'Look What You Made Me Do With This Bucket', the only track from the abandoned project that was salvaged for inclusion on *Reputation*.

Swift was reportedly disappointed with the final recordings and ate them, infuriating over-weight middle-aged male commentators the world over.

■ **HEAR IT:** Bootlegged copies of *Bucket* are rumoured to circulate on the dark net, but it's probably best to wait until the T-Swizzle releases her note-for-note re-recorded version of it.

Venetian Glass Bucket

'Guido! I wanna bucket made of glass.'

'Whaddya ya mean, Benedetta, made of glass? Donna be idiota. Glass is forra window, orra glass "chin chin bottom up, ol' fellow", orra nice a-spade. No forra bucket.'

'I wanna bucket made of glass, Guido, and I wan it here inna Venice with canal anna gondolier anna dolphin.'

'I know we in Venice, Benedetta – we live here twenny year, since 1730. Same palazzo.'

'Then why we speak together in stereotype of Italian speaking in Inglish, Guido? We both Italian.'

'I know, Benedetta. Let's a-stop anna speek in Italian with – I donna know how say – *sottotitoli*.'

'*Bene, è un sollievo.*'

(Well, that's a relief.)

'*D'accordo. Allora, perché l'impulso improvviso per un secchio di vetro?*'

(Too right. So, why the sudden urge for a glass bucket?)

'*Ne ho visto uno a casa di Alessandra. Giuro che ha tenuto solo quella festa per poterla sfoggiare.*'

(I saw one at Alessandra's house. I swear she only gave that party so she could show it off.)

'*Ma si romperà, mia cara! Non appena ci versi del cemento!*'

(But it will break, my dear! As soon as you pour cement into it!)

'*Mamma mia! Non è per cemento. Ti aspetti che io abbia una festa qui senza una adesso? La mamma diceva sempre che avevo sposato un deficiente …*'

(My mother! It's not for cement. You expect me to have a party here without one now? Mother always said I'd married a moron …)

■ **SEE IT:** British Museum, London. They've got shedloads of them. In the mid-19th century you couldn't move for collectors dying and bequeathing their Venetian glass buckets to the museum. Well, OK, it was Sir William Temple and particularly Felix Slade, a solicitor who was mad for them and wanted the nation to share in his madness (but only after he'd got safely out of the way first).

US Navy K-G Underwater Cutting-Equipment Bucket

A lot of otherwise mild and unopinionated people howl, 'No no no, buckets shouldn't go underwater.' They throw their hands in the air in what is, for them, a rare act of despair, and declaim, 'It's *unnatural*.'

As strange as it may seem – given that Uncle Sam's armed forces are famous throughout the globe for taking into account the concerns of others – the US Navy pays no heed to those people. Also, the mariners do have history on their side. Since the planet's first roughly cylindrical open-topped containers were created over four millennia ago by the Bucket People (short-lived rivals of the Beaker Folk whom the larger vessel producers considered very precious and la-di-da-too-refined-to-drink-out-of-a-bucket-snooty-hoots), buckets have been submerged for all manner of reasons. Just ask the bucket at any well or the Tongan thunder prawn trawling bucket.

Indeed, it was the capacity of the bucket to survive full immersion that inspired Navy scientists to put underwater cutting equipment in one. For decades, Navy divers had been obliged to carry their cutting equipment in their hands or pay small children to dive alongside them and pass them the tools at the appropriate moment. So when the K-G Underwater Cutting-Equipment Bucket became standard issue, American underwater cutting took off in a big way. Soon divers were cutting all kinds of things below the waves: fish, cables, seaweed, colleagues – if it was underwater it was considered fair game. Underwater Demolition Teams were established in World War II so that once things were cut up they could then be blown up 'because that would really show 'em'.

The lack of a lid naturally meant that most of the equipment floated away within minutes (see also Moon-Landing Rock Sample Bucket p5) but that just created more stuff to be cut up, so it was win-win really.

■ **SEE IT:** The Smithsonian, Washington DC, USA.

The Bargain Bucket

'The horror! The horror!'

One of the most fondly cherished stories that has come out of the 19th-century literary realm – perhaps second only to the revelation, long after his death from fur balls, that Hilaire Belloc once ate all of Elizabeth Gaskell's wigs as a dare – is the fact that Joseph Conrad found the inspiration for Kurtz' final words in *The Heart of Darkness* by imagining his hero going into a shop and taking the foolhardy decision to look into a bargain bucket.

Also known as the 'bargain bin', 'bargain basket' or 'open sewer', the bargain bucket is the living embodiment of the wash-out, the fiasco, the débâcle, the flop. Indeed, not merely the flop but the mega-flop, the snafu, the ultra-dud, the über-meh. For these, my friends, are the products that have *failed*. They came into the shop full of hope and promise but have found themselves unloved, unwanted and, ultimately, unsaleable. Books, obscure cleaning products, moustache dispensers, rocket launchers, unicorn-shaped glitter, more books – they are all sucked into the black hole of despair and self-loathing that is the bargain bucket.

And though admittedly such wares can be picked up at ludicrously knock-down prices, the real cost becomes apparent when you get home and find you are now the owner of a hardback edition of a volume of whale-meat recipes ghost-written for a former Big Brother runner-up. And since doing Nowhalemeatvember you don't even *like* whale meat.

■ **SEE IT:** Frankly, you'd be advised not to. However, if you must, remember that it's extremely dangerous to look directly into a bargain bucket – instead, take a hand-mirror and view the bucket from an oblique angle. Never attempt to operate heavy machinery while under the influence of the bargain bucket and always make sure you have a friend waiting outside with smelling salts, transport and a mallet.

ABANDON
HOPE ALL YE
WHO ENTER
HERE

Ned Kelly's Bucket Helmet

Australian outlaw Ned Kelly is, of course, best known for his famous catchphrase, 'Don't call me Harry!'

For decades after his execution in 1880 for being quite naughty 'even by Australian standards', the saying was widely believed to be a reference to the Australian slang term 'Harry', meaning 'a person obsessed with the whinging Poms'. This characteristic eventually became so common in Australians that to call a citizen of the knuckleduster-shaped country a 'Harry Aussie' became a tautology and the word fell into disuse.

Nowadayser historians are cleverer than previous incarnations of the profession and have realised that this interpretation of Kelly's words is completely erroneous. The cheeky larrikin was instead railing against the charge often made against him by rival hoodlums and ne'er-do-wells that by adopting an upside-down bucket as a helmet, he was merely aping the fatally-flawed tactic employed by Harold II of England (see p41).

This nettled the bushranger and aesthete. As he would explain to his detractors over his favourite bottle of eucalyptus wine, 'I'll own there's some truth in the assertion that I have re-visited the late Anglo-Saxon monarch's notion of the *soi disant* bucket-as-helmet. However, the modifications I have made – the bullet-proof thickness and that majestic wrap-around crown-piece with its pencil-thin eye-slit – echo more the stylings of Edward III than of Saxon England (just run your finger along that gorget, my friend – it's a masterpiece of the blacksmith's craft). So to say that I have slavishly copied the helmet-bucket of 1066 is to defame my good name and, should you persist, I shall regrettably have no other option but to seek remedy in the courts …

… Just kidding!'

And then he would shoot them in the eyes.

■ **SEE IT:** State Library Victoria, Melbourne, Australia.

Stanislas Sorel's Galvanised Bucket

'Papa, I want to make something of myself.' The small boy ran his finger nervously along the workbench in his father's poor and miserable clockmaker's shop.

'Oh Stanislas, that's no way to talk. Why can't you be happy taking on the family firm and being a poor and miserable clockmaker? After all, you were born here in Putanges – a village whose name you will have to pronounce very carefully for the rest of your life. And people will still snigger.'

But little Stanislas Sorel would not be persuaded. When he grew up he would become a metallurgist! And not any old metallurgist but the finest metallurgist France had ever seen. He would work with iron, with steel, with

119

zinc ... with many other kinds of metal he couldn't think of right now because of the pressure of the moment and his father's weird eyebrows and because he was still thinking of Putanges and why folk would snigger at the name. Copper! That's another one. He would work with copper. And calico! Was calico a metal? Probably. And assuming it was he would definitely work with it. Unless it turned out to have inherent weaknesses or was mined unethically, that is. And he wouldn't stop until he had patented coatings for billiard balls. *And* invented artificial stone, because the DIY warehouse stores of the future would sell any old tosh. And to top all this, he would find fame throughout the world for his work of terrifying brilliance: the World's First Galvanised Bucket! *Mais oui, papa!*

Also, he had already made up his mind to tell people he was from Caen.

■ **SEE IT:** Pretty much everywhere. If there are at least twenty things in your line of sight right now, the chances of one of them *not* being a galvanised bucket are practically nil. Tick it off right now and move on to a trickier one.

Bucket 'n' Spade Bucket

It's an established fact that the most important cultural function of the bucket 'n' spade bucket is to introduce children to the contemptibly pointless world of work.

Often presented with the equipment before they've even learnt to walk or master the subjunctive, the benighted infant is cajoled into filling the bucket with sand, the essential quality of which makes it wholly unsuited for use as a principal building material. The mewling tyke is then pressed upon to upturn the bucket, tipping its newly quarried contents straight back onto the beach. If the vessel is a high-concept 'castle keep' design, the likelihood of all the sand being released from its grasp is pretty much nil, especially if said sand is damp. Bashing the bottom of the bucket with the spade to loosen the non-compliant residuum inevitably results in

123

a broken spade, a broken child and/or moist sand flying off in all directions, invading sandwiches, ice creams, every injudiciously open orifice in the vicinity, and mother's glass of lemonade into which she has surreptitiously slipped a generous measure of gin (a measure that events will prove insufficient).

Should the puling tot's architecturally-deficient assemblage reach the point at which it can be conferred with the title 'sandcastle' it awaits two possible fates. The edifice will either be flattened and stricken from the Earth by the advancing waves or, if built beyond the tide's reach, simply abandoned at the end of the day to wither away in the insensate wind or be trampled into nothingness by the heedless hooves of the unthinking masses. Either way, the exercise is rendered senseless and devoid of purpose. If the child also identifies with the grains of sand, bereft of agency and driven hither and yon by mere whim and circumstance, the lesson is complete.

■ **SEE IT:** Head for your nearest sandy beach – the noise of children weeping as they take their first horrified look into an inexplicably meaningless future will direct you bucketwards.

The Marlborough Ice Pails

'Pounced, moulded, incised, chased.'

We've all had days like that. If it's any consolation (though admittedly no sentence that starts that way ever was), so too did this pair of ice pails, according to the Keeper of the Pails at the British Museum. The only difference between them (the pails, not the Keeper) and you (you) is that they're about 320 years old, made of pure gold and were designed to be able to stand up with a bottle of wine inside them.

Weighing in at 365 troy ounces and 6 pennyweights (p131), if you melted them down you could exchange the gold for a half-decent ocean-going yacht or the toe of a top footballer. Not that you'd want to melt them down because then you'd lose their Huguenot-influenced spiral gadrooned decoration and, more to the point, a rare

125

opportunity to say 'gadrooned', the drunk form of the word 'dragooned'.

The pails once belonged to Sarah Churchill – Duchess of Marlborough, Princess of Mindelheim and Countess of Nellenburg – or, as she's better known, Rachel Weisz in *The Favourite*. She bequeathed them to the Honourable John Spencer, which meant they were never inherited by her husband's descendant, Winston Churchill. This is as well because he would in any case be embroiled in a bucket-related incident all of his own (p147). Instead, the Spencers kept them at Althorp until 1981. This is the same year that one of the Spencer daughters married someone called Prince Charles. Coincidence? Or just two events that happened in the same year? Either way, the ancient law that anyone whose bottle of chardonnay fits either of the pails will be immediately crowned as the new British head of state is tested each Lammas Day. Entry costs a pound.

■ **SEE IT:** British Museum, London. If you've had no luck with your bottle of chardonnay, cheer yourself up with a gander at the museum's Venetian Glass Buckets (p107). Being a monarch's rubbish anyway.

Leonardo da Vinci's Gyro-Bucket

L ike most people living in the late 15th and early 16th centuries, Leonardo da Vinci was obsessed with the problem of how to make buckets fly. This was no frivolous pursuit but arose from the pressing need in those days to find out if water, when lifted high enough into the air, would burst into flames and turn to gold. Water was fairly plentiful in late 15th- and early 16th-century Vinci while gold was not, and the town's citizens felt that a transposition of even a moderate quantity of Adam's ale into shiny ingots would raise their prospects no end.

Da Vinci was never one to shrink from a challenge. He was, after all, the man who first discovered a use for broccoli. Sitting at his gyro-desk (an earlier da Vinci invention but only capable of flights up to ankle height), he sketched the nocturnal hours away. His first attempts were, it must be said, disappointing: a camel forced to drink gallons of water, fitted with wings and urged skyward by men with prongs; a huge whale-skin hand filled with water and raised to the heavens by a flock of trained skylarks; and one idea that doesn't seem to have got further than the scrawled words 'goat trampoline?'

Legend has it that Leo was eventually inspired to design the gyro-bucket when he saw a peasant woman hurl a situla (see p23) at a dishonest kelpmonger and was impressed at the missile's aerodynamic properties. Being a genius, he simply thought up the gyro bit himself. The oddest thing about the story is that water *does* actually catch fire and become gold if lifted high enough. The government doesn't want us to know though so has covered it up.

■ **SEE IT:** Museo Nazionale della Scienza e della Tecnologia Leonardo da Vinci, Milan, Italy (ask for the '*giro-secchio per favore, un cappucino con paraorecchie marce e un pugno nei capelli*').

The Bucket as Unit

When was the last time someone rang you up and said, 'Hey, do you fancy going out tonight and measuring a few things?'

Some while back I would hazard, for it must be admitted that although modern times have given us the smart phone, the laser beam and the plague, the merriment has largely been excised from the once cheery business of quantifying. The British insistence on weighing themselves in stones, the pub landlady's lingering fondness for the gill and firkin, and the racecourse owner's penchant for the furlong are but pale shadows of the bacchanal of delights once enjoyed by the men, women and children of yore.

'Who's on for a noggin?' one would declaim before falling into a cauldron of catmint and drowning.

'Four bushels to the coomb!' a merchant would cry, shamelessly parading his book learning, for he was the first in the town to have learnt the alphabet all the way to *J*.

The drachm, the sock, the strike, the wey, the perch, the ell – they all had their place in the once-colourful world of volume and distance. But the monarch among all these was the bucket, around which all other units of capacity revolved. If you wanted two pecks of hock for your child's party, half a bushel of paraffin for a witch-burning, or a quarter strike of helium to liven up the drearier sections of your pilgrimage to Rome, you'd order a bucket's worth and heaven help the tradesman who sold you a minim or a scruple short.

Today, if you're seized by a sudden and all-consuming yen for a bucket of strychnine, on sallying forth to your local apothecarist you must perforce request 32 pints, four gallons or 18.185 litres of the cheeky little alkaloid. No wonder everyone nowadays looks sad all the time.

■ **SEE IT:** Musée des Arts et Métiers, Paris, France.

Wellington's Bucket Fountain

ew people would deny that the bucket is the apogee of sculptural achievement, the towering summit of artistic creativity beyond which the human hand cannot, indeed, *durst not* go for fear of bringing down the wrath of gods jealous enough at seeing mortal beings swanning about with buckets without being provoked any further by the creation of some even higher expression of the sculptor's art.

So when, in 1969, a duo called Burren and Keen got together with Graham Allardice (not, as his name would suggest, the somewhat balding and corpulent fellow in accounts whose personal hygiene routine could do with a spritzing but whose way with a purchase order makes him essential to the smooth running of the organisation, but an architect) to create a work of kinetic art in (*drum roll*) 'the first pedestrian mall in all of New Zealand', many looked on with eyes anxiously turned towards the heavens.

Thankfully, rather than being all fancy-dan high-concept god-wrath-inducing, the fountain turned out to be a bit of a laugh. Water fills a bucket until it tips, launching its contents vaguely towards the next bucket down but, more impishly, mainly over passing pedestrians. Kiwis have little to do when not travelling abroad so enjoy spending their time adding washing-up liquid to the fountain's water, or filling it with fake blood (or what is *probably* fake blood), or stealing the buckets, or returning the buckets, or simply getting splashed. There's never a dull moment.

Indeed, if you visit New Zealand and haven't been splashed by Wellington's Bucket Fountain, you haven't visited New Zealand. Even if you have, and you met one of Flight of the Conchords and took a selfie with him while bellowing 'Band meeting!' instead of 'Cheese!', you still haven't, I'm afraid. Life is hard.

■ **SEE IT:** Cuba Mall, Cuba Street, Wellington, New Zealand.

Archimedes' Bucket

Not to be confused with the unfairly maligned Pythagoras' Bucket (p47), Archimedes' version was principally a Bucket of the Mind™. It happened first in his mind, which was fortunate, because his was the kind that could do something about it rather than thinking, as so many of us would, 'What's that bucket doing in my mind? Be gone, rapscallion vessel, so I can get back to thinking about swans.'

In his corpse-packed stab at Scandi-noir, *On Floating Bodies*, Archimedes posited that 'any object, totally or partially immersed in a liquid, experiences an upthrust equal to the weight of liquid displaced by that object'. This made him something of a hit at parties, particularly if he brought his bucket along to demonstrate and the

hostess could furnish him with a body of water, a length of rope and a rudimentary pulley system.

'I solved a problem for the king with this,' the doughty little Sicilian would say as he was setting up the mechanism.

'Ah yes,' the party-goers would respond en masse, 'we'd heard he suspected a goldsmith of mixing some silver with the gold he'd been given to make a crown in order to trouser, by which of course we mean toga for the trouser is yet unknown to us, a volume of gold equal to that of the silver. '

And by the time they'd finished their sentence, the bucket would be ready for lowering.

'You see,' Archimedes would begin, 'it's all about density equalling mass over volume.'

'And what's this we hear,' the spell-bound party-goers would ask while a quantity of a liquid denser than water filled the bucket, 'about you leaping from your bath and running through Syracuse starkers?'

'Ah, that,' Archimedes would reply, 'well happily the king made all the charges just sort of go away.'

And there would be a low muttering that Archimedes would ignore.

■ **SEE IT:** Museo Leonardo da Vinci (p129) e Archimede, Syracuse, Sicily, Italy.

The War of the Bucket's Bucket

O to have lived in one of Italy's myriad city states in the Middle Ages. The tiny fiefdoms fought each other tooth and nail, the ever-regurgitated enmity passed down through the generations like a genetic disposition to a septic knee or a clinically-interesting bile disorder. The neighbouring city states of Modena and bigger badder Bologna were no exception. The latter constantly bragged about having invented spaghetti bolognese, while the burghers of Modena waved their bottles of balsamic vinegar about, which was also rude.

Then there was the whole Pope thing. If you counted yourself a Guelph (and the Bolognese did), you loved that old Pope, whoever he (or she) happened to be. However,

if you'd nailed your septic knee to the Ghibelline mast (as
had the Modenese) you very much dug his rival, the Holy
Roman Emperor (particularly his earlier less commercial
work). After a century or so of fighting, the reasons for
killing each other had become a bit fuzzy. So, in 1325, the
good yet violent folk of Modena had an idea: they'd spark
off a proper reason for a war. Quick as a reasonably fast
horse, they popped over to Bologna and stole the city's
bucket, thus making their opponents' well look a bit ridic.
Cue mayhem.

Or at least, in an ideal world, that's what *would* have
happened. In fact, a glance at the timeline of the so-called
War of the Bucket reveals that Inter Balsamic beat their
eternal foe at the Battle of Zappolino *before* celebrating
by nicking their enemies' pail, known thenceforward
as *La Secchia Rapita* (The Kidnapped Bucket). For the
Guelphs and the Ghibellines, the bucket-snatching
actually demonstrated that the war was on its last legs. Just
204 years later, a truce was declared.

■ **SEE IT:** As befits a bucket, Modena's Palazzo Comunale
has a whole room devoted to it. If that doesn't sate your
bucket-ardour, a faithful imitation hangs high up in the city's
Ghirlandina tower.

Aboriginal and Torres Strait Islander People Kelp Water-Carrying Bucket

Merseyside: home of The Beatles, The Beatles Museum, The Beatles Experience, The Beatles Walking Tour and the Scouse accent, a distinctive mode of pronunciation in which, among other curiosities, the letter k is pushed so far back into the throat that it sounds like the 'ch' in loch.

Listen carefully to The Beatles' 1965 Lennon-scribed smasheroo 'Help!' and this knowledge suddenly gives the song a previously unrecognised complexity. Far from being a plea for assistance, the then moptop's tune is rather a paean to kelp, the large brown algae seaweed

that grows to an enormous size, creating virtual forests beneath the waves. Lennon explains that in his youth he never felt the need for anybody's kelp but now he realises the error of his ways and he's open to offers of the iodine-rich seaweed from all possible sources. Such is his new-found appreciation for kelp that, in a paroxysm of ecstasy, he over-reaches himself and starts to use it as a verb. McCartney apparently objected to this quite violently but was forced to the ground by Harrison and Starr, and then over-ruled in a band vote.

More than anyone else, the Aboriginal and Torres Strait Islander People of Tasmania would have understood Lennon's kelp-love. Their particular genius was to look at the heterokont seaweed and think, 'Yes, that's the solution to my water-transportation problems.' By fashioning a kelp bowl and adding a couple of sticks and some plaited river reed for the handle, they had a bucket in which they could carry water wherever they liked – even up and down stairs.

The entire indigenous population of Tasmania was wiped out by British settlers in the 1800s. No liquids of any sort have been conveyed anywhere on the island ever since. Ask for some water in Tasmania today and you'll be presented with a straw and given directions to the nearest river.

■ **SEE IT:** Tasmanian Museum and Art Gallery, Hobart, Tasmania, Australia.

The Yalta Conference Bucket

'Oh those Russians,' mused Germano-Caribbean philosophers Boney M on their 1978 Euro disco hit 'Rasputin', neatly typecasting an entire nation by extrapolating from one extreme example. And never did the Russians prove themselves to be more Russian, at least in the Boney M interpretation of the word, than at the Yalta Conference of February 1945.

The summit can best be understood as a sort of stag do gone horribly wrong at which the participants, rather than ransacking Prague dressed as Sponge Bob Square Pants, set about divvying up the entire post-war world. Somewhere around day three, with tempers fraying over the future of the Soviet Union's freshly-acquired chunks of Poland and American president Roosevelt's insistence on looking ill all the time, thus killing the mood, Joseph Stalin played his master stroke: he had Churchill's ashtray replaced with a bucket. This not only meant that Winston had no further excuse for missing the target with his cigar residue, it also had the effect of making him appear smaller relative to the now vastly enlarged ash receptacle. The newly diminished Churchill swiftly gave in to Stalin's demands, cementing Soviet hegemony over eastern Europe for decades to come. The only downside for the Russian leader was that Roosevelt, mistaking the bucket's purpose, kept being sick into it (see also p35).

It's surely no coincidence that neither of the two guests would ever recover from what would henceforth be known unofficially as the Ash-Vom Bucket Conference. Roosevelt died shortly afterwards. Churchill completely lost his marbles, wandering around proclaiming 'Keep England White', like some sort of Fortnum & Mason Enoch Powell. Stalin, meanwhile, just carried on killing people in their millions. Oh those Russians indeed. Except that he was Georgian.

■ **SEE IT:** The Vladimir Putin Museum of Vladimir Putin's Favourite Manly Things, Putinsburg, Russia.

Schrödinger's Bucket

Theoretical physicist Erwin Schrödinger's famous cat-in-a-box was not his first attempt to produce an easily cranially-digestible thought-experiment for the masses. Such is made plain by his diary entry for 3rd November 1934:

'Imagine a bucket half-filled with custard of a density that may or may not sustain the weight of a flailing kitten. Until you look into the bucket you do not know whether there is a live kitten inside still happily thrashing about on the surface of the custard or a dead kitten submerged beneath the yellowy lacto-depths, or indeed a kitten both alive *and* dead, flailing and non-flailing, merely custard-bespeckled and yet custard entombed also.'

Having experimented with various densities of custard and degrees of feline thrashiness (using such a prodigious quantity of increasingly angry kittens that *Felis catus* became locally extinct in Austria – there are still shortages to this day), Schrödinger at last felt he had got it, in his words, 'Just right.'

It was only when his great friend Arthur Schopenhauer pointed out to him that a kitten flailing about in custard lacked the necessary gravitas to convey the point at which quantum superposition ends and reality disintegrates into two distinct and irreconcilable possibilities, that Schrödinger bought up a job lot of boxes and began his much more dignified experiments with sources of radioactivity, Geiger counters and flasks of poison. And cats.

To be honest, it's probably best to leave this bucket until last. The smell, they say, is something awful.

■ **SEE/NOT SEE IT:** The final 'just right' bucket of kitten-o'-custard is on permanent display in the Erwin Schrödinger International Institute for Mathematical Physics in the physicist's home city of Vienna, Austria. Or perhaps it isn't. Until you visit the institute etc. etc. …

Acknowledgements

Naturally, a work of such preeminence does not come into being without the selfless and unwavering industry of a highly skilled team.

I'm thus very thankful to my crack research squad who fearlessly dedicated their lives to this venture:

Olivia Wills (Wellington consultant), Mathilde Croziat (linguistic adviser), Jackson Hunt (linguistic advice fixer), Edwin Wills (thinker of things), Clive Wills (thinker of other things), Proper Steve (historical chaplain), Jones the Opinion (knower of stuff), Jon Payne (keeper of baseball nerds) and Sauro Scarpelli (Italian virtuoso).

I'm deeply grateful to Kim and Nick Hoare at Ivy Grange Farm, Suffolk, in whose shepherd's hut I wrote half this book and whose delicious meals sustained me through the livelong day.

Thanks be to my friendly agent Michael Alcock at Johnson and Alcock.

Many thanks to Rory Walker for his excellent illustrations which bring to the buckets the dignity and nobility they so richly deserve.

An appreciative wave to Duncan Heath at Icon for badgering me into writing this long overdue encomium to the great buckets of the ages. Thanks are also due to Sara Bryant for proof reading the book and ensuring it contains not a single misprunt.

And finally, I'd like to record my gratitude for the fine work of Ellen Conlon at Icon, for whom I know the editing of this volume is the fulfilment of a lifetime's ambition.